TORNADOES

SEYMOUR SIMON

HarperCollins*Publishers*

PHOTO CREDITS
Permission to use the following photographs is gratefully acknowledged:
pages 5, 23, Photo Researchers, Inc., © Howard Bluestein;
pages 6–7, National Severe Storms Laboratory/Phil Degginger/Color-Pic, Inc.; pages 12–13,
Joseph H. Bailey, © National Geographic Society; page 15, NWS/Birmingham, AL; page 17,
Chris Johns/National Geographic Image Collection; pages 18–19, NOAA/Corbis; pages 20–21,
E. R. Degginger/Color-Pic, Inc.; page 25, National Center for Atmospheric Research, Boulder,
CO/Harald Richter; pages 26–27, 28, 31, © Jim Reed; page 32, NOAA, National Severe Storms Laboratory.

Art on page 9 and both maps on page 11 by Ann Neumann.

The text type is 18-point Garamond Book.

Library of Congress Cataloging-in-Publication Data
Simon, Seymour.
    Tornadoes / Seymour Simon.
        p.   cm.
    Summary: Describes the location, nature, development, measurement, and destructive effects of tornadoes, as well as how to stay
out of danger from them.
    ISBN 0-688-14646-5 (trade) — ISBN 0-688-14647-3 (lib. bdg.) — ISBN 0-06-443791-4 (pbk.)
    1. Tornadoes—Juvenile literature.   [1. Tornadoes.]   I. Title.
QC955.2.S56   1999   98-27953
551.55'3—dc21   CIP
                                                                                                                  AC

Visit us on the World Wide Web!
www.harperchildrens.com

Twisters, dust devils, whirlwinds, waterspouts, cyclones—tornadoes go by different names. But whatever they are called, the roaring winds of a tornado can toss a truck high into the air, smash a building, and snap the trunk of a tree like a matchstick.

A tornado's funnel looks like a huge elephant's trunk hanging down from a cloud. The funnel acts like a giant vacuum cleaner—whenever the hose touches the ground, it sucks things up into the air.

Tornadoes (from the Spanish word *tronada,* meaning "thunderstorm") have been reported in every state of the United States and in every season. However, they occur most often in the eastern two-thirds of the country during the spring, which is sometimes called tornado season.

To Chloe's new brother, Jeremy Scott, with love

A tornado is a powerfully twisting column of air that makes contact with the ground. It is visible when it contains water droplets in the form of a cloud, or surface dust and debris, or some of both. When a tornado touches down, it usually creates an explosion of dust and wreckage on the ground. If the twisting column of air does not touch down and does not produce damage, it is called a funnel cloud.

Most tornadoes are local storms. A typical tornado

is four hundred to five hundred feet wide, less than a thousand feet long from cloud to ground, and has winds of less than 112 miles per hour. It usually lasts only a few minutes and covers only a few miles on the ground. But a few monster tornadoes are a mile wide and have the strongest winds ever measured in nature: up to 300 miles per hour. They can last for an hour or more and travel more than two hundred miles along the ground, leaving enormous damage in their wake.

The first step in the birth of a tornado is usually a thunderstorm. This type of storm begins when warm, humid air rises upward from the ground. As these updrafts cool in the upper atmosphere, the moisture in them forms clouds. The water droplets or ice crystals in the clouds grow bigger as water vapor around them condenses, or becomes liquid. The droplets or crystals begin to fall, creating downdrafts, and these downdrafts meet new updrafts, which continue feeding warm humid air into the spreading thunderhead cloud.

This is the most violent time in a thunderstorm. A tornado may form at the edge of an updraft, where it meets a downdraft. The updraft pulls air away from the ground, which creates an area of low pressure. More air rushes in to take the place of air that's been pulled up. Then the falling water droplets in the downdraft get swept in and begin to form the tornado's funnel-shaped cloud. As the swirling winds pick up dirt from the ground, the funnel grows darker.

There is a continual battle across North America between large bodies of air called air masses. Air masses can be cool or warm, moist or dry. For example, cool dry air comes from northern lands, while warm moist air comes from the Gulf of Mexico and the Pacific Ocean. Air masses push each other across the lines where they meet, which are called fronts.

As a cool air mass presses forward, it slides underneath a warm air mass and pushes the warm air up. Fast-growing clouds called thunderheads take shape along the front and storms develop. A squall line made up of several thunderstorms may be more than one hundred miles long.

Sometimes a large thunderstorm, called a supercell, forms on the southwestern end of a squall line. Supercells often develop spinning winds inside them called mesocyclones. Some die out after a few minutes, while others spin faster and form funnel clouds at their bases. The strongest tornadoes form in the updraft areas of mesocyclones.

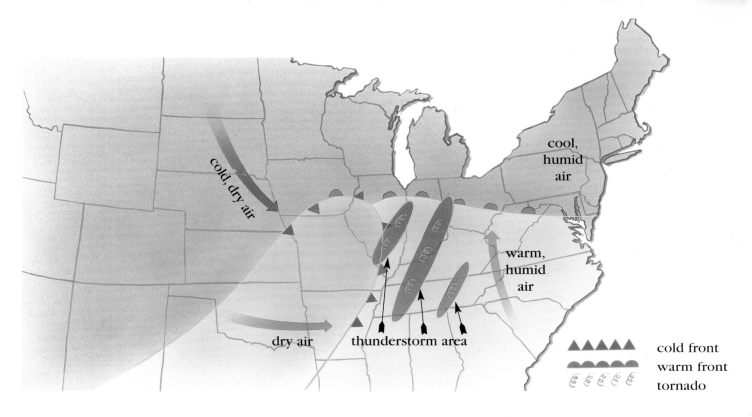

cold, dry air

cool, humid air

warm, humid air

dry air

thunderstorm area

▲▲▲▲▲ cold front

⌒⌒⌒⌒ warm front

tornado

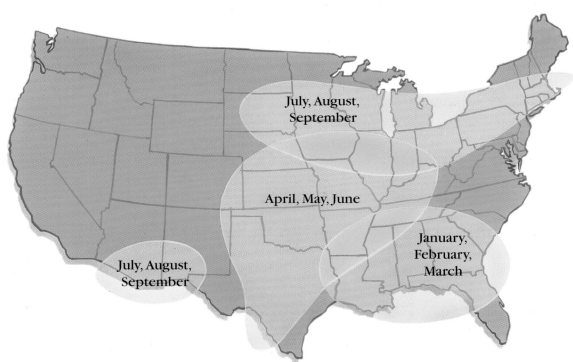

July, August, September

April, May, June

January, February, March

July, August, September

Supercells are most common between April and June. And they are most likely to occur in an area known as tornado alley, which runs from central Texas as far north as Illinois and Indiana and as far east as Kentucky. From January to March, supercells form in some southern states, and from July through September, they can occur in the southwest and the northeast.

Tornadoes born in supercells are hugely powerful. One monster tornado that touched down in Illinois in 1990 lifted a twenty-ton trailer truck from a highway and bounced it up and down like a ball before depositing it in a field eleven hundred feet away. A strong tornado can pick up a house and move it down the block to another lot.

Sometimes tornadoes do odd things. A tornado once sucked up a pond full of frogs and rained them down on a nearby town. Another tornado struck a house and carried a five-hundred-pound piano twelve hundred feet through the air.

One of the worst tornadoes of recent years struck the town of Jarrell, Texas, on May 27, 1997. A thunderstorm came rumbling out of the north in the middle of the afternoon. Moving at a slow 20 miles per hour, the storm entered the town, and several twisters dropped out of the clouds. One resident later said, "That sky was black as night, just boiling."

The largest tornado moved slower and stayed longer; it sat on the ground for fifteen to twenty minutes, destroying everything it touched. The twister sucked trees out of the ground and pulled up nearly a mile of the road leading into town. Driving rain and hail came behind the twister. Survivors opened their eyes to see dark sky where their roofs had been.

By the time the tornado left, fifty homes had been lifted up and smashed down and twenty million dollars of damage had been done to the small town. Twenty-seven people had died, out of a population of one hundred thirty-one.

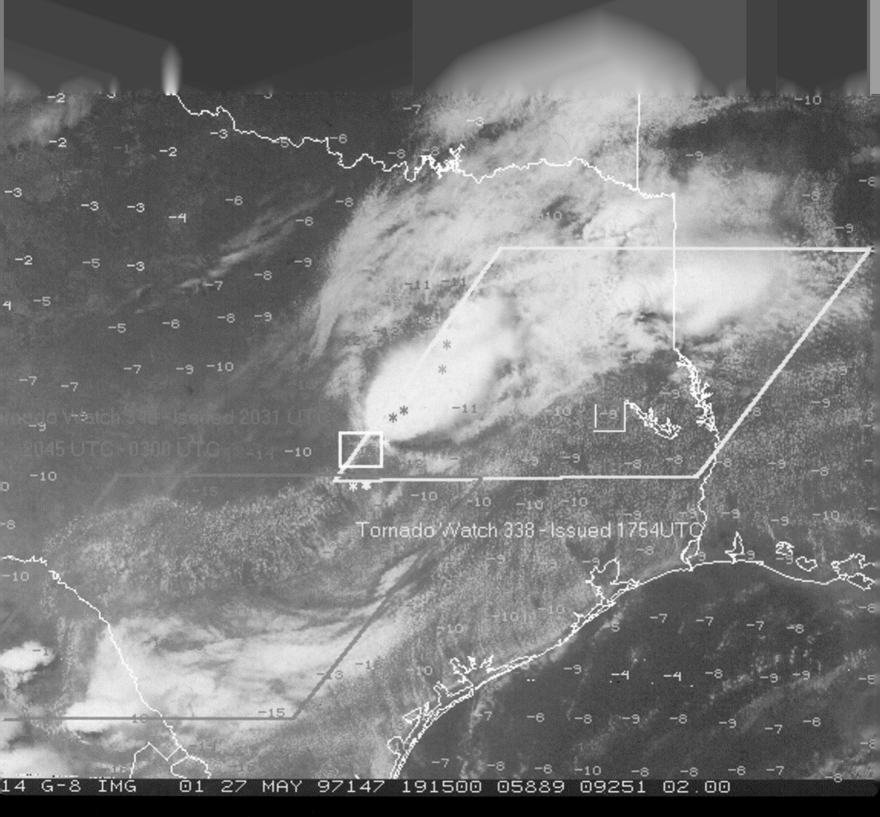

This is a Doppler radar photograph of the area around Jarrell, Texas, on May 27, 1997. The asterisks show the location of tornado activity. The asterisk in the white box in the center marks the location of the monster tornado that hit Jarrell.

The single deadliest tornado in history was the Tri-State tornado. It touched down in Missouri on March 18, 1925, in the early afternoon, and swept into Illinois and then Indiana. It sounded like "a thousand freight trains."

The Tri-State tornado traveled along a 219-mile path of death and destruction. In three and a half hours, the tornado killed 689 people, injured 2,000, and left more than 10,000 homeless.

Most tornadoes come singly, but sometimes many travel together. In early April 1998 a line of tornadoes along a thunderstorm ripped through one little town after another in Mississippi, Alabama, and Georgia. The monster tornadoes destroyed hundreds of homes, schools, and churches and caused dozens of deaths. Some people were even sucked out of their homes. Rescue workers compared the destruction to that of a bomb blast.

Fortunately, not all tornadoes are as violent and destructive as the Tri-State tornado of 1925 or the April 1998 tornadoes. Most tornadoes are much weaker.

The Fujita-Pearson Tornado Intensity Scale (or F-Scale) ranks tornadoes according to their wind speed and the kind of damage they can cause. Weak tornadoes are classed as F0 or F1 and are much more common than strong tornadoes. F0 tornadoes have winds that range from 40 to 72 miles per hour. They do light damage to chimneys, TV antennas, and roof shingles. Small tree branches can be broken. Nearly three out of every ten tornadoes are classed as F0.

Slightly greater damage is caused by F1 tornadoes. These storms have winds of 73 to 112 miles per hour. They can uproot some trees, overturn automobiles and small trucks, and push trailers around on the ground. About four out of every ten tornadoes are in the F1 class.

Waterspouts are weak tornadoes that form over warm water. This is a photograph of a waterspout on the ocean. Waterspouts are most common along the Gulf Coast and in the southeastern states.

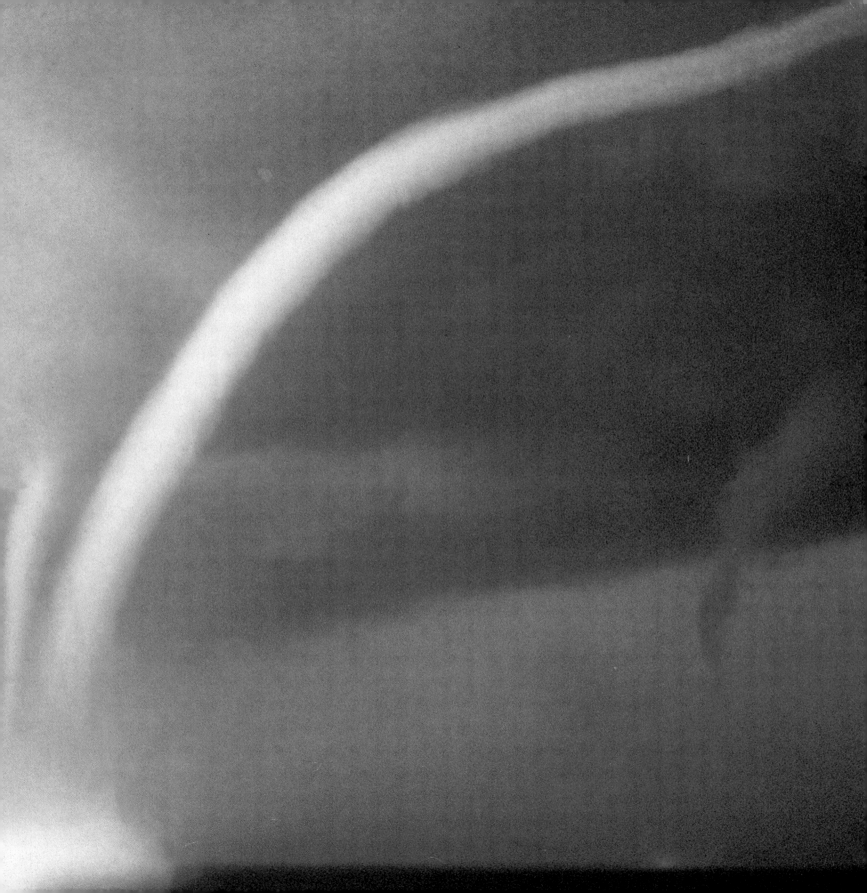

Strong tornadoes are classed as F2 and F3. F2 tornadoes have winds of between 113 and 157 miles per hour. They cause considerable damage. F2 tornadoes may blow roofs off homes, leaving only strong walls standing. They demolish sheds and small outbuildings. They can overturn mobile homes and cause walls of wooden buildings to collapse. About two to three of every ten tornadoes are classed as F2.

F3 tornadoes cause severe damage, since they have winds ranging from 158 to 206 miles per hour. These tornadoes can flatten all the trees in a forest and collapse metal buildings. They blow off roofs and tumble exterior walls made of concrete blocks. Six out of every hundred tornadoes are classed as F3.

This photograph shows an F3 tornado that hit Marmaduke, Arkansas, in March 1997. It destroyed eleven homes, damaged fifty-seven others, and resulted in one death. The tornado followed a nearly straight line one hundred yards wide and a mile long.

The most violent tornadoes are classed as F4 or F5. An F4 tornado has a wind speed of 207 to 260 miles per hour. Such powerful winds will leave few if any walls standing, even in sturdily built apartment houses. F4 tornadoes can pluck trees up from their roots and break their trunks in half. They can pick up and throw large building materials long distances, hurling them with such force that the materials penetrate concrete. Only two out of every hundred tornadoes are classed as F4.

F5 tornadoes—the highest classification on the F-Scale—are the monster tornadoes. Their winds blow at speeds of more than 261 miles per hour. They can cause incredible damage, including leveling almost any small or medium-sized building and making the land look as if a bulldozer roared across it.

The F5 tornadoes are the rarest. Fewer than one out of every hundred tornadoes is classed as F5. The Tri-State and Jarrell, Texas, tornadoes are examples of how destructive an F5 tornado can be.

Learning about tornadoes can help to save lives. For example, even though the average tornado travels at 30 miles per hour, much faster ground speeds—up to 70 miles per hour—have been reported. That means that trying to flee to safety in an automobile may be reasonable in the country, where the roads are not crowded. But in populated areas, traffic-clogged roads can make it dangerous to get into an automobile.

It is also untrue that tornadoes never strike big cities. For example, Nashville, Tennessee, was badly damaged by a violent tornado in April 1998. And in the past forty years, St. Louis, Missouri, has been hit by tornadoes more than twenty times.

Still another myth is that opening the windows in a house will help prevent it from being destroyed by a tornado. In fact, opening the wrong windows could allow air to rush in and blow the structure apart from inside. The best advice is to forget the windows and get to a shelter.

One of the most important things you can do to prevent injury in a tornado is to be alert to the onset of severe weather. Learn the signs of approaching bad weather, so that you will know to tune in the weather forecasts on TV or radio. If a tornado watch is issued for your area, it means a tornado is possible, because one has already been spotted either on the ground or on radar.

Here are some of the things people hear or see just before a tornado arrives:

•The sky turns a greenish or greenish black color.

•There is a sound a little like rushing air or a waterfall, and it turns into a roar as the tornado comes closer.

•Debris drops from the sky.

•A funnel-shaped cloud appears. It is spinning, while other clouds are moving very quickly toward it.

If a tornado watch or warning is posted, then a real danger sign that a tornado is coming is falling hail.

It is also a good idea to know, *before* a tornado strikes, where to go for shelter. Cars and trailers are *not* safe during a tornado. Go to the basement of a solidly built house. Staying under the stairs or a heavy table helps to protect you from crumbling walls. Blankets can also help to shield you from flying debris.

In an apartment or a home without a basement, an inside room or closet is the safest place. Getting into a bathtub and putting a couch cushion over you helps protect you on all sides. Bathtubs are usually solidly anchored to the ground and sometimes are the only things left in place after a tornado hits.

If you are out walking or biking and are caught in the open when a tornado touches down, lie flat in a ditch or low area if there is *no* rain. If there *is* rain, there may be a danger of flash flooding. Then you should take shelter away from trees and power lines and away from glass windows or doors in houses. Crouch down and make yourself as small a target as possible.

Weather scientists, called meteorologists, are trying to find the best ways to predict and warn against tornadoes. One thing they do is to keep a close watch on severe thunderstorms. They also look for a wall of clouds, which can spawn a tornado. The National Weather Service uses Doppler radar, which can show air movement as well as the shape of clouds. Early signs of rapid air rotation during a thunderstorm can allow life-saving warnings to be issued fifteen to twenty minutes before a tornado forms.

Each year about a thousand tornadoes touch down in the United States, far more than in any other country in the world. Only a small number actually strike occupied buildings, but every year hundreds of people are killed or injured. The chances that a tornado will strike you or a building that you are in are very, very small, though. In fact, you are about as likely to be hit by lightning or to be the victim of a shark attack as to be struck by a

The best protection from tornadoes comes from receiving an early warning. Listening to local radio or television stations during a weather watch can alert you to take safety measures as soon as a tornado warning is broadcast. You don't have to worry too much in advance about tornadoes, but finding out when they are coming and knowing what to do is certain to help you if one strikes.

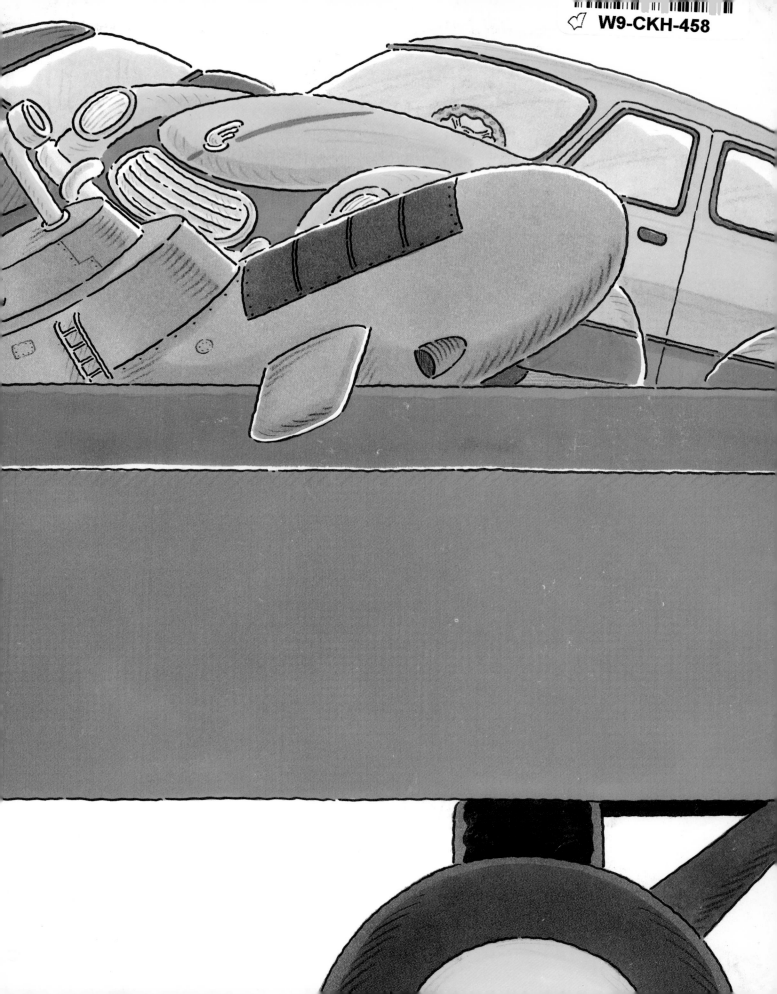

First Questions and Answers about **Transportation**

Why Are Wagons Red?

TIME
LIFE for
Children ®

ALEXANDRIA, VIRGINIA

Contents

Why are wagons red?

Wagons used to come in different colors: red, blue, yellow, green, and white. As time passed, people seemed to like red ones best, so that's the color most wagons are today.

Wheee!

4

5

Why are wheels round?

So they can roll! A wheel's round shape makes it easy to roll. That makes things with wheels easy to push or pull.

Try it!
Put a round ball and a square block on the floor. Give each one a push. Which goes farther?

Why do tricycles have three wheels?

Three wheels make a tricycle easy to ride. When your feet turn the pedals, the wheel in front moves the tricycle forward. The wheels in back keep it from falling over.

I wish I could be a bulldozer!

9

How do people ride bicycles without falling over?

It takes a lot of practice. If a bicycle is standing still, it falls over. But when a bike is moving forward, it stays up. Riders must learn to sit carefully on bicycles so they don't lose their balance. Two extra wheels, called training wheels, can help you learn to ride a bike.

Did you know?
Always wear a helmet when you ride a bicycle. The helmet will protect your head if you fall.

Do bulldozers doze?

No, they work hard! A bulldozer goes where there are no roads. It rolls over rocks, through mud, and up and down steep mounds of dirt. A bulldozer runs on two tracks. Each track is stretched around two large wheels. When the wheels move, the tracks turn and the bulldozer goes forward. A bulldozer weighs more than 10 elephants, but the tracks keep it from sinking into the ground.

Whew! This is hard work!

Did you know?
The tracks of a bulldozer are called caterpillar treads because they look like crawling caterpillars when they move.

Why do trains run on tracks?

Train tracks are a special kind of road. The wheels of a train fit neatly onto the tracks. When the train rolls forward, the tracks give it a smooth ride.

15

Why do train cars look different?

Because they do different jobs!

Sand, grain, coal, and other loose loads go in a **hopper car**.

A **coach car** carries people.

16

A **gondola** carries heavy things like steel pipes and concrete blocks.

Flatcars move heavy things—even bulldozers!

Don't forget me— I'm the caboose!

An **engine** drives the train.

What makes cars go?

Every car has an engine inside it.
The engine works with other
parts of the car to make it go.

Your body needs food to move your arms and legs. In the same way, the engine of a car needs gasoline to move the car's wheels. When the wheels start turning, the car rolls forward.

Did you know?
Always buckle your seat belt when you get inside a car. That way you won't get hurt in a sudden stop.

What are all those knobs and dials for?

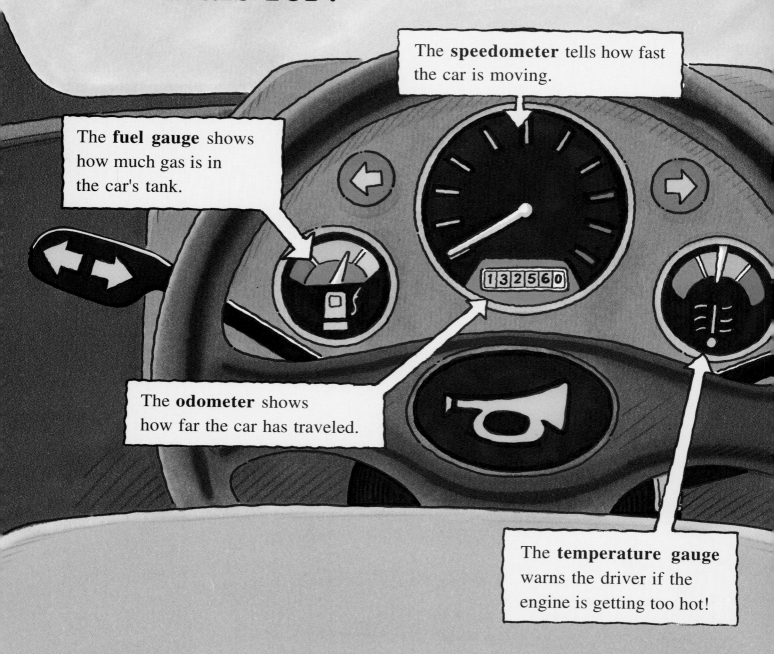

The **speedometer** tells how fast the car is moving.

The **fuel gauge** shows how much gas is in the car's tank.

The **odometer** shows how far the car has traveled.

The **temperature gauge** warns the driver if the engine is getting too hot!

The knobs turn on everything from the heater and air conditioner to the radio and windshield wipers. The dials tell the driver how the car is running.

20

What do big trucks carry?

Big trucks are like railroad cars. They carry many different things.

A **dump truck** hauls sand, gravel, and dirt. The back tips up for unloading.

Moving vans carry furniture when people move to a new home.

A **flatbed truck** hauls heavy loads like big machines and boats.

A **car carrier** takes new cars from the factory where they were made to the store where they are sold.

A **tank truck** brings gasoline to the gas station.

Get me down from here!

23

What makes a boat move?

Many boats have a motor that works like the engine of a car. But a boat's motor does not move wheels–it moves a propeller. The propeller has blades that turn around and around. When the propeller spins, it pushes the boat through the water.

Why are some ships so big?

Big ships carry things across wide oceans.
They do different jobs.

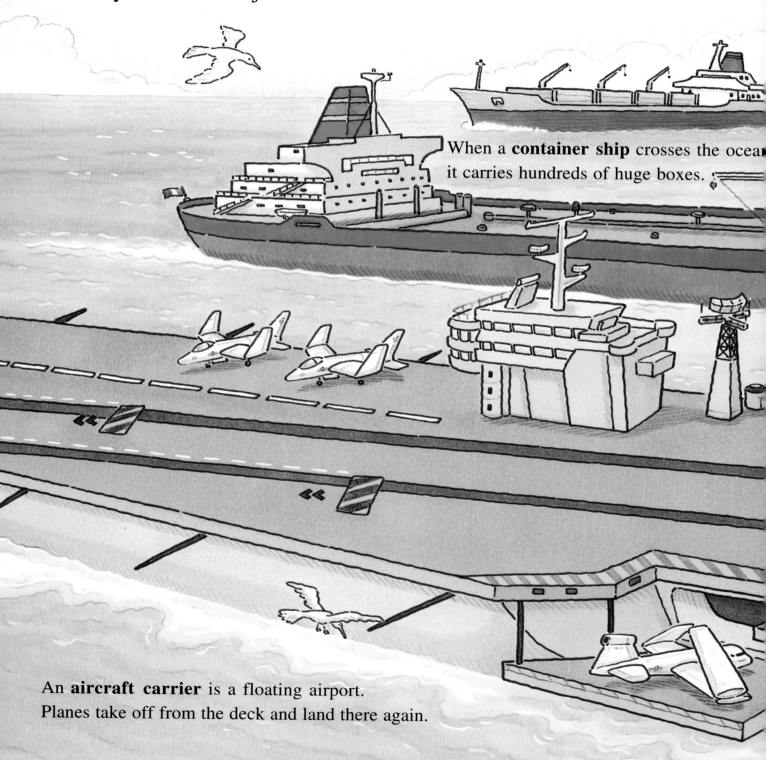

When a **container ship** crosses the ocean
it carries hundreds of huge boxes.

An **aircraft carrier** is a floating airport.
Planes take off from the deck and land there again.

An **ocean liner** carries many people. Like a small city, it has everything that people need: stores, restaurants, movie theaters, bedrooms, and bathrooms.

Supertankers are filled with oil. They are the largest ships of all.

27

How do tall ships go under bridges?

Most bridges have room for tall ships to float under them. But some bridges have a special section that lifts up to make way for big boats. People who want to cross the bridge must wait until the boat sails through.

Do people live on boats?

Yes, they do. A houseboat is a wide, flat boat that has a kitchen, a bathroom, a living room, and a sun deck. Most of the seats on a houseboat turn into beds. Houseboats are usually docked in one place, where the water is very calm.

Did you know? Some people eat, sleep, and work on underwater boats called submarines.

Going down!

What makes submarines go underwater?

A submarine has special tanks that make it go up and down. When the tanks are filled with water, the submarine gets heavier than the water around it and sinks. When the tanks are emptied, the sub grows lighter and rises to the surface.

Try it!

With a parent's help, put the lid on an empty container and set it in water. Does it float? Now fill the container with water. Replace the lid and put the container back in the water. What happens?

33

How do hot-air balloons go up and down?

When the air in a balloon is heated, it becomes lighter than the air around it, and the balloon rises. When the air inside cools down, the balloon slowly lands. Hot-air balloons don't have engines; they float wherever the wind takes them.

Did you know?
A blimp is a big balloon with an engine and a propeller. A pilot steers the blimp through the sky.

How do airplanes fly?

Airplane wings are curved on the top and flat on the bottom. When a plane is moving, air goes faster over the top of the wings. It goes slower beneath the wings. When that happens, the air above the wings sucks the plane upward, and the plane flies through the sky.

What is a helicopter?

A helicopter is an aircraft with giant blades on top.
The blades are shaped like thin airplane wings.
When the blades spin quickly, they lift the helicopter
into the air.

Did you know?
Helicopters can stay still, or hover, in midair. They can land in small areas, like a rooftop or a lawn.

How far do spacecraft fly?

Spacecraft fly very fast and very far. After a spacecraft blasts off from earth, computers guide it into space. Some spacecraft have flown farther than the moon, the sun, and the farthest planets.

...3, 2, 1, Blastoff!

Did you know?
In space everything is weightless.
Astronauts float, rather than walk,
inside the spacecraft. They can
even sleep upside down!

41

Are there roads on the moon?

No, there aren't. Nobody lives on the moon. When astronauts went to the moon, they took a special car with them. They drove this lunar rover across the dust and rocks that cover the moon.

Did you know?
When the astronauts left the moon, they had to leave the lunar rover behind. If you went to the moon, you would still see it there.

43

Why do spacecraft fly around the earth?

Spacecraft that go around and around the earth are called satellites. Most of them do not carry people. Instead, they send information to earth. Some satellites take pictures of the planet. Others report on the weather. Satellites help people see television pictures from other parts of the world.

44

How does the space shuttle come back to earth?

First, it has to slow down! In space, astronauts use the shuttle's rocket engines to make it go slower. Then the shuttle comes back into the air around the earth. In the air it flies like a big glider. The astronauts steer it down to a smooth landing in the desert.

It's great to be back home!

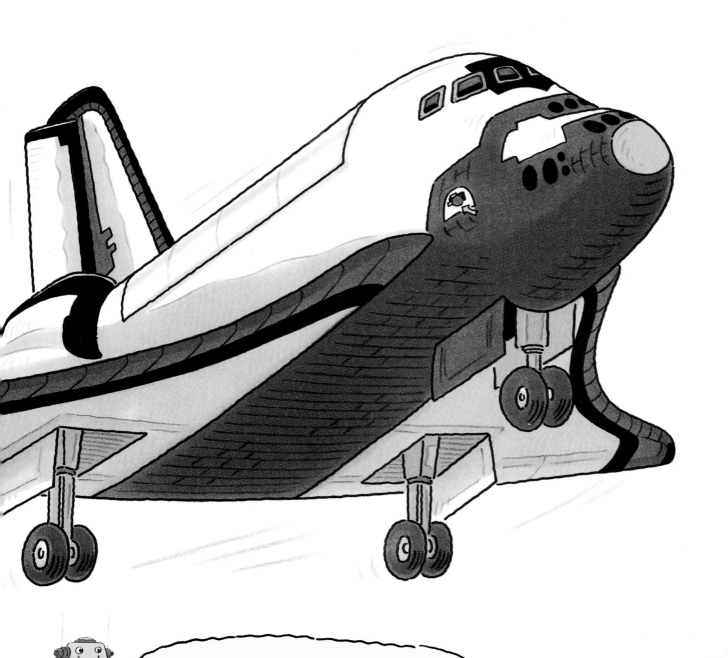

Did you know?

The space shuttle does not take off like an airplane. It blasts straight into the air with the help of big booster rockets.

TIME-LIFE for CHILDREN ®

Managing Editor: Patricia Daniels
Editorial Directors: Jean Burke Crawford, Allan Fallow,
　　　　　　　　　　Karin Kinney, Sara Mark , Elizabeth Ward
Editorial Coordinator: Marike van der Veen
Administrative Assistant: Mary M. Saxton
Production Manager: Marlene Zack
Senior Copyeditor: Colette Stockum
Production: Celia Beattie
Supervisor of Quality Control: James King
Assistant Supervisor of Quality Control: Miriam Newton
Library: Louise D. Forstall, Anne Heising

Special Contributor: Barbara Klein
Researcher: Marike van der Veen
Writer: Andrew Gutelle

Designed by: **David Bennett Books**
Series design: David Bennett
Book design: Andrew Crowson
Art direction: David Bennett & Andrew Crowson
Illustrated by: Steve Cox
Additional cover
　illustrations by: Nick Baxter

First printing. Printed in U.S.A.
Published simultaneously in Canada.

Time Life Inc. is a wholly owned subsidiary of THE TIME INC. BOOK COMPANY.

TIME-LIFE is a trademark of Time Warner Inc. U.S.A.

For subscription information, call 1-800-621-7026.

School and library distribution by Time-Life Education,
P.O. Box 85026, Richmond, VA 23285-5026.

Library of Congress Cataloging-in-Publication Data

Why Are Wagons Red?: first questions and answers about transportation.
　　　p. cm. — (Time- Life Library of first questions and answers)
　　　ISBN 0-7835-0878-6. — ISBN 0-7835-0879-4 (lib.)
　　　1. Transportation — Miscellanea — Juvenile literature.
　[1. Transportation — Miscellanea. 2. Questions and answers.]
　　　　1. Series: Library of first questions and answers.
　　　TA1149. W49 1994　　　　　　　　94-2054
　　　629. 04— dc20　　　　　　　　　　CIP
　　　　　　　　　　　　　　　　　　　　AC

Consultants

Dr. Lewis P. Lipsitt, an internationally recognized specialist on childhood development, was the 1990 recipient of the Nicholas Hobbs Award for science in the service of children. He has served as the science director for the American Psychological Association and is a professor of psychology and medical science at Brown University, where he directed the Child Study Center from 1968 to 1993.

Dr. Judith A. Schickedanz, an authority on the education of preschool children, is an associate professor of early childhood education at the Boston University School of Education, where she also directs the Early Childhood Learning Laboratory. Her published work includes *More Than the ABCs: Early Stages of Reading and Writing Development* as well as several textbooks and many scholarly papers.